Dedication

We dedicate this project to our families.

About the Authors

R. Brad Althouse has been a researcher with the Center for Persons with Disabilities at Utah State University since 1985. With a background in education and computer science, he has opportunities to apply a wide variety of technologies to educational needs. In addition to his previous work with computer-assisted training and computational programs, his latest projects involve using the Internet for data instruction.

Dr. Bill Jenson is a professor and chair of the Educational Psychology Department at the University of Utah. He is the former director of the Children's Behavior Therapy Unit, a day treatment center and school for autistic and behavior disordered students in Salt Lake City. Dr. Jenson is a nationally known presenter and published author of a number of books, including *Understanding Child Behavior Disorders* and *Managing the Noncompliant Child*, and is a co-author of *The Tough Kid Book*. He has also published dozens of journal articles and book chapters.

Marilyn Likins is a Research Specialist for the Technology Division, Center for Persons with Disabilities at Utah State University. Prior to graduate school, Dr. Likins worked for seven years as a behavior specialist at the Children's Behavior Therapy Unit (CBTU) for Salt Lake Mental Health. Dr. Likins has a strong background in special education teacher and paraprofessional preparation, classroom and schoolwide management, social skills training, effective instructional practices, and distance education.

Dr. Daniel Morgan received his bachelor's degree in special education at Western Michigan University, his master's degree in special education at Michigan State University, and his Ph.D. in special education from Florida State University. He has been on the faculty in the Department of Special Education and Rehabilitation at Utah State University since 1976. His professional interests include effective programs and services for students with behavior disorders, personnel preparation in special education, substance abuse prevention for students with disabilities, and legal issues in special education.

Contents

Introduction

Get 'Em On Task: A Computer Signaling Program to Teach Attending and Self-Management Skills

General Overview: *Get 'Em On Task* is a computer program that helps teachers create an individualized auditory signal system for monitoring student behavior to make sure the students are on task and improving academically. You can use this system with an individual student or group of students in grades K-12 to support any positive reinforcement or self-management program. A variety of options for using the system are discussed in the Classroom Management Programs section of this manual.

This program is flexible and can be easily tailored to meet your needs. By following step-by-step instructions, you can set how long the program will run, set the number of signals, determine whether they will occur randomly or on a regular schedule, and vary how the signals will sound. To provide added incentive for your students, you can create "bonus" signals by making some signals worth more than others.

This manual is divided into three basic sections: (1) the computer program and its installation and functioning; (2) a system to assess on-task behavior and several management approaches that can be used in classrooms; and (3) the Appendix containing materials discussed in the Management Programs.

Computer Program

Program Installation and System Requirements

Minimum system requirements:
- Windows 98/Me/NT®/2000/XP
- MAC OS® 8.6 to MAC® X10.X
- Pentium II processor or Power Macintosh Power PC (G3 or higher recommended)
- 32MB RAM & 320MB available disk space
- 8X CD-Rom drive
- 16-bit-color display
- Sound Card

1. Insert the installation CD into optical drive (CD-Rom).

2. Get 'Em on Task Setup Wizard
   A. Windows
      1) The Get 'Em on Task Setup Wizard should start up automatically. If it does not, navigate to your optical drive, right click "Open," and click the "Setup" icon.
      2) Click the "Next" button
      3) The Additional Task screen will open. Click the "Next" button.

4) The Ready to Install screen will open. Click the "Install" button.

5) The Completing Get 'Em On Task Screen will open. Click the "Finish" button.

*If you do not want Get 'Em On Task to launch after installation finishes, de-select the check-box option.

B. Mac OS (No installation required)

Running the Program

1. If you are using Windows:

    A. Double-click on the Get 'Em On Task icon located on your desktop.

    B. The introductory screen will show. Click the "OK" button.

2. If you are using Mac OS:

    A. Click the CD Get 'Em On Task icon located on your desktop.

    B. Click on the Get 'Em On Task folder.

    C. Click on the Get 'Em On Task icon.

    D. The introductory screen will show. Click the "OK button."

Introduction Screens

Get 'Em On Task

A Computer Signaling Program to Teach Attending and Self-Management Skills

R. Brad Althouse
William R. Jenson, Ph.D.
Marilyn Likins, Ph.D.
Daniel P. Morgan, Ph.D.

Ok

Get 'Em On Task   SOPRIS WEST

Welcome to Get 'Em On Task: A Computer Signaling Program to Teach Attending and Self-Management Skills to Children and Youth.

Get 'Em On Task helps you to create an individualized beep or signal system. You can use this system to support any positive reinforcement or self-management program.

This program is flexible and can be easily tailored to meet your needs. By following step by step instructions, you can set how long the program will run. You also can set the number of signals, whether they will occur randomly or on a regular schedule, and vary how they will sound.

To provide added incentive for your children or students, you can create "bonus" beeps by making some beeps worth more than others.

Ok

Get 'Em On Task   SOPRIS WEST

The Main Screen

This is the screen where you enter the information regarding when and how often you would like the program to signal. Once you enter how long you want the program to run, you can then enter how many signals you want during that period. After you have entered the number of signals, the program lets you choose between randomly and evenly placed signals. You may also enter the number of points associated with a standard (nonbonus) interval and the number of bonus intervals you want to have. A bonus interval provides additional motivation because it's worth double the points of a standard interval. You can vary the possible number of points for the period by changing how much a standard interval is worth and by changing the number of bonus intervals. When you are finished changing the settings, click on the "View Schedule" button so that you can check the spacing of signals and the placement of bonus intervals on the View Schedule screen. Then click on the "Back" button to return to the Main Screen. If you're not satisfied with the random placement of the bonus signals or the lengths of the intervals, you can either have the program reschedule by clicking on the "View Schedule" button again, or you can change some of the numbers on this screen and again click the "View Schedule" button. Repeat this procedure until you are satisfied with the signal placement.

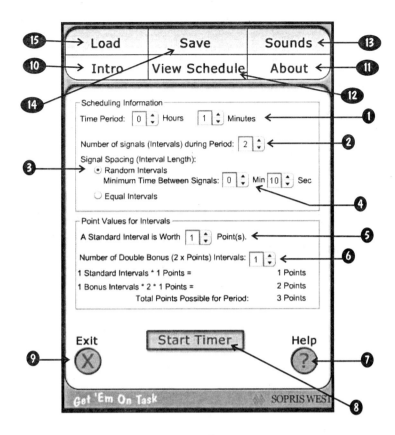

You can Exit the program by selecting the "Exit" button.

You can set up and test your sound setup on the "Sounds" screen.

1 Use these fields to set the number of hours and/or minutes in the signaling time period.

2 Use this field to tell the program how many signals you want during the time period.

3 Select either Random or Equal Intervals between signals.

4 If you want a minimum time period between signals, use these fields to specify the minimum interval.

5 Tell the program how much a standard interval is worth here.

6 Tell the program how many bonus intervals to have here.

7 Click here to display help on how to use this screen.

8 Click here if you're satisfied with the schedule and are ready to start the signaling period.

9 Click here to quit the program.

10 Click here to view the Intro screen.

11 Click here to view About information.

12 Click here to view and have the program schedule the signals and points.

13 Click here to change the signal sounds.

14 Click here to save a schedule.

15 Click here to load a saved schedule.

Help on Setting the Signal Schedule and Point Values

On the Main Screen, you must tell the program: (1) how long to run; (2) how many signals to give; (3) how to space the signals; and (4) the total number of points that can be earned during the period.

First, fill in the hours and/or minutes for the time period you want the program to run.

Next, fill in the number of signals you want the program to give during this period. See the Classroom Management Programs section of this manual for help in determining how many signals to have during a given period.

Third, decide whether you want the signals to be evenly spaced or randomly spaced. Click on the radio button (the little circle) next to the spacing type you want. Note: If you choose to space the signals randomly, you can also enter a minimum interval time. This will keep the signals from coming too close together. However, the number you enter may be reduced if there are too many signals to space that far apart.

Finally, enter the number of points that can be earned during this period. Start by entering how much a standard interval will be worth. Next, enter how many bonus intervals (double points) you want to have during the period. Notice that when you enter these numbers, the total number of possible points is calculated for you. You can change the number of signals, the value of a standard interval, and the number of bonus signals until you get a total that fits your needs.

The limits for the fields are:
    Time Period—Hours: 0–8
    Time Period—Minutes: 0–59
    Number of Signals: 0–100
    (no more than 1 for every 10 seconds is allowed)
    Standard Interval Points: 1–100

When you have entered all of the information, click on the "View Schedule" button. The program then creates a schedule of when the signals will be given and how much each interval is worth. You are shown a different screen where you can view and print the schedule. Leave this screen by clicking on the "Back" button.

You may want to listen to the signals that the program is going to give. To do this, click on the "Sounds" button. Make any necessary changes and click the "OK" button. Refer to "The Sound Source Screen" section of this manual for more details.

If the schedule meets your needs, click on the "Start Timer" button to begin the timer program. The Progress Screen will appear, showing the timer counting down.

If the schedule is not satisfactory, make changes to the information on the Main Screen and then click on the "View Schedule" button to recalculate the schedule and points.

The Schedule and Point Values Screen

This screen summarizes the signal schedule that resulted from your instructions. It indicates when the signals will occur and which ones will be bonus signals. If you are satisfied with the schedule, click on the "Back" button. If you would like to change the signal tones or sounds, click on the "Sounds" buttons. Return to the Main Screen to start the program. Click on the "Start Timer" button when you're ready to begin. The Progress Screen will allow you to monitor the signaling process.

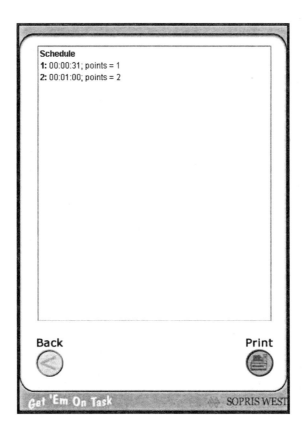

The Sound Source Screen

This screen can be reached from the Main Screen by selecting the "Sounds" button. It allows you to select the source of the signal that will be used to indicate the end of an interval. In addition, the signal can be modified and tested.

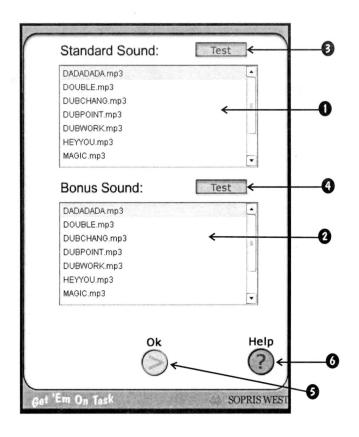

❶ Select sound for Standard Sound.

❷ Select sound for Bonus Sound.

❸ Test Standard Sound.

❹ Test Bonus Sound.

❺ "OK" button to return to Main Screen.

❻ "Help" button to view the Help Screen.

The Progress Screen

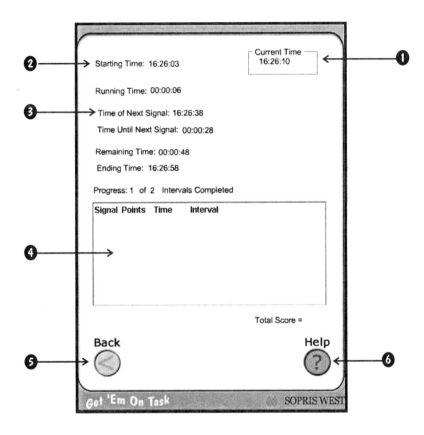

This screen allows you to monitor the progress of the program.

❶ Tells you the current time.

❷ Shows you when the program was started.

❸ Tells you when and how soon your next signal will occur.

❹ Shows a record of the session. Each interval and the points associated with it are shown. Also listed are the starting and ending times and whether the program was paused.

❺ This button stops the program and returns to the Main Screen.

❻ "Help" button to view the Help Screen.

Classroom Management Programs

Selecting Reinforcers and Developing a Menu

Selecting appropriate reinforcers for use in this program is critical to its success. The first rule in choosing reinforcers is that they should not take a lot of time or cost a lot of money. The second rule is that you should ask for the students' input. What do they want that does not take a lot of money or time? The third rule is to THINK LIKE A KID. The problem with most reinforcers is that teachers assume they know what students want, but they look at the situation from an adult's perspective. The fourth rule is that variety is very important. Even the best incentive loses its value if it is used too often. The fifth rule reflects research that shows that adult praise is one of the most important reinforcers that students (yes, even secondary students) want. In using this program, it is important to pair awarding points, Yes cards, or any other tangible reinforcer with verbal praise.

In the Appendix of this manual you will find lists of reinforcers that elementary and secondary students generally like, and a Reward Menu that you can laminate and use to list reinforcers with a water-based pen (so you can change the rewards periodically).

Remember—What You Reinforce Is What You Get

Before using this program, it is very important to recognize that simply rewarding on-task behavior probably will not improve academic performance in a classroom. Research indicates that what you reinforce is what will improve. To make this program work most effectively, you should reinforce both on-task behavior and academic improvements. The point system presented later in this manual shows how to reinforce both. Similarly, if you use the Yes and No program, the Beat the Number program, or any of the self-management programs, you need to also reward academic performance. For example, one easy way to do this is to simply collect all the assignments during a period where you have been using the signaling program, shuffle the assignments, and randomly select three. Without indicating which three students' papers have been selected, immediately grade them. If they meet your criteria (e.g., 80% correct, all problems tried), then proceed with your selected reinforcement program (e.g., selecting a card from the Yes and No container). If the papers do not meet your requirements, then do not use the reinforcement program.

Assessing On-Task Behavior in Your Classroom

This section gives you two basic methods for assessing on-task behavior in your classroom. The first method is an easy and fast approach that can be done in any classroom. The second method is a more sophisticated one that can be used for research or more formal requirements.

Is it necessary to measure on-task behavior before you use the *Get 'Em On Task* program? No, the program can be run successfully without any assessment measure of on-task behavior. However, it is easy to forget how much a student or classroom has improved without some type of baseline measure. Additionally, if there are formal requirements for a measure such as teacher and student performance evaluations, a requirement for documenting the improvement of on-task behavior as described in a student's IEP, legal demonstrations of on-task behavior, or research questions, then a baseline measure of on-task behavior may be necessary.

Method One: Easy Method

1. Define on-task behavior as "eyes on teacher" or "appropriate materials required."

2. Tell the class you want to start a new signal computer program, and you will be running it during a certain subject (e.g., math, reading, or a required in-seat assignment). You should probably pick a time of day when you suspect on-task behavior is at its lowest and is a big problem.

3. Play the computer signal program for two or three days until the students are used to the computer signal (it is best to use the signal for this assessment period and not the human voice). If a student asks you why there is a signal playing, indicate it is a project for yourself and at this time the class should not pay any attention to it.

4. Use a Point Card, with squares numbered 1–30 (located in the Appendix), for each student.

5. On the fourth day (or when the students are used to the program), set the number of signals at 10 or 20 signals per hour.

6. When a signal sounds, scan the classroom, and if any student is off task, put a minus sign (–) in one of the squares on the card. If they are all on task, put a plus sign (+) on the card. At this time, do not say anything to the students, just collect the data.

7. After two to three days of collecting data, add up the number of plus signs you have marked and divide it by the total number of signals you have played over the number of assessment days. Then multiply this number by 100. This yields your percentage of on-task behavior (e.g., the total number of pluses (30) divided by the total number of signals (60) multiplied by 100 = 30/60 x 100 = 50% on task).

Method Two: Response Discrepancy Method

This is a more formal method and allows a comparison of your most problematic student to the whole class in terms of on-task percentage. It is called a response discrepancy method because it shows how discrepant the least on-task student is from the whole class average for on-task behavior.

1. Use the Behavior Observation Form located in the Appendix.

2. Get the class used to the signals as described in Method One.

3. Set the number of signals to 90 signals, use a standard interval (not random), and use a 15 minute period of time. A signal will sound every 10 seconds.

4. Decide which student has the most difficulty with staying on task.

5. Familiarize yourself with the student behavior codes listed on the Behavior Observation Form.

6. When a signal sounds, look at the target student (the one with the most difficulty staying on task) and also at a same-sex peer.

7. If the target student is on task, put a + in the box. If he or she is off task, put the appropriate code in the box. Make the same determination for the same-sex peer.

Using a Mystery Motivator in the Classroom

A Mystery Motivator is an easy way to deliver an incentive either to the entire classroom or to an individual student.

Materials

An envelope and a blank piece of paper.

Steps

1. Select some basic rewards for the students for use as Mystery Motivators. For hints, watch what students do frequently (this is what rewards them), keep track of what they ask you for, ask them for reward suggestions, use a menu or checklist, or look in the back of this manual at the lists of reinforcers. Make a list of at least 10 rewards that do not take a lot of time or cost a lot of money. It helps to think like a student while generating this list.

2. Write one selected reward on a piece of paper and put it in an envelope. Seal the envelope and do not tell the students which reward you chose. If you are working with one student, it may help to staple or tape the envelope to the student's activity. If you are using the Mystery Motivator with the whole class, it helps to tape the envelope in the front of the room. **Technique Hints:** Draw question marks on the envelope, refer to it, point to it during the day, give the students hints about what is inside (e.g., it is brown and awesome).

3. Define the behaviors you want the student(s) to increase. This definition should be objective and specific. If you cannot see the behavior or measure it, then it is probably a bad choice (i.e., improve your attitude, be more responsible, be a good citizen, or do better work are all poor general choices). Some good specific choices include: being on task and working, being in your seat ready to work before the bell, finishing your assignment with at least 70% accuracy, breaking no classroom rules, handing in your homework, good lunchroom behavior (no food on floor, not being disruptive), good report from the bus driver, etc.

Using a Reinforcement Spinner in Your Classroom

A Reinforcement Spinner is a circle with different sized numbered pie wedges and an attached arrow that can be spun (see example in the Appendix).

Steps

1. Have the students help you select five reinforcers. Have them rank the reinforcers from most preferred to least preferred.

2. Laminate the spinner on poster board. Cut out the arrow and attach it to the spinner with a small metal brad.

3. List the reinforcers on the Reward Menu (located in the Appendix) using a water-based pen (it helps to change one or two reinforcers weekly). The most preferred reinforcer should be listed as #2 on the menu which corresponds to the smallest wedge of the pie on the spinner. The second most preferred reinforcer should be on the next smallest wedge, and so on. The reason for this type of placement is to have the most valued reinforcers be the hardest to get. This allows you to use some relatively expensive or time consuming reinforcers that will not be frequently given.

4. When the criteria are met (e.g., number of points earned, a Yes card pulled, or a Secret number beaten), the arrow on the Spinner is spun and the number it points to corresponds to the reinforcer that the class will get for that day.

The Yes and No Management Program

This program is designed to be used with the *Get 'Em On Task* program, a series of Yes and No cards, and a Mystery Motivator (or Reinforcement Spinner). Each time a signal sounds, scan the classroom. If everyone in the class is on task and working, put a Yes card into a container. If one student is off task or not working, put a No card into the container. Near the end of the day, ask a student to draw a card out of the container without looking. If the card is a Yes, the whole class gets to do the Mystery Motivator. If a No card was drawn, the class continues with an academic subject. Take all of the cards out of the container and start the process over the next day.

Materials

Yes and No cards (blackline master located in the Appendix), an opaque container (like a plastic pitcher), and a Mystery Motivator or Spinner (blackline master located in the Appendix).

Steps

1. Laminate the Yes and No cards and cut the cards apart. The number of cards needed is approximately double the number of scheduled signals, in case all observations lead to a Yes or to a No determination (i.e., 10 signals require 20 cards).

2. Make a Mystery Motivator. Use an envelope with a question mark on it and a piece of paper inside listing the reward. Seal and hang the envelope on the bulletin board or blackboard.

3. Have the students generate some ideas for the Mystery Motivator (e.g., 15 minutes free time, having a story read to them, watching a video, popcorn party, etc.). **Hint:** Have the students generate about 20 Mystery Motivators, about a month's supply (5 really good ones and 15 good but common ones). Write the 20 incentives on pieces of paper, put them in the envelopes, and mix them up. Then use them during the next month. This enhances the anticipation because no one is sure which Mystery Motivator is going to be chosen.

4. Each time a signal sounds, scan the classroom and decide whether all the students are on task and working or if they are not. If they are all on task, put a Yes card in the container. If they are not, put a No card in the container. **Optional:** If you program bonus signals, put two Yes cards in the container if the students are on task and only one No card if they are not.

5. At the end of the day (during the last 15–30 minutes), have a student draw a card from the container. If it is a Yes card, take down the Mystery Motivator and do what the reward indicates inside. If it is a No card, continue with the regular instruction. **Variation:** For secondary students, Fridays (half or full period) can be used for the Mystery Motivator day. The program is used all week without emptying the container, and then a card is drawn on Friday.

6. The next school day, have a student sort the cards into two piles (one for Yes cards and one for No cards) and start the system again. If necessary, put up a new Mystery Motivator.

7. Start the system using 10–15 signals per hour, and slowly reduce the number of signals to 2 or 3 when the system is operating well.

8. **Caution:** If one student is intentionally setting the class up to get many No cards, do not let that student participate for two days. While the other students are enjoying a Mystery Motivator, this student should work on an academic assignment until he or she can participate in the system fairly.

The Get 'Em On Task Program With a Point System

This program utilizes the *Get 'Em On Task* computer program with a point system in the classroom. Each time a signal sounds, scan the room. If all the students are on task and working, tell them to mark a point on their Point Card. If a student is off task, instruct that student (by name) to mark an X (no points) for that interval, and instruct the rest of the class to mark a point on their individual cards.

Materials

A Point Card for each student (blackline master located in the Appendix), a classroom bank (blackline master located in the Appendix) where points are recorded and saved by students, and a reward store with the cost in points for each reward.

Steps

1. Ask the students what they would like to earn in a classroom store. These items should include special activities, privileges, and treats (e.g., edibles such as a can of soda, small toys like stickers or a white elephant, items brought in by teachers). A good store should contain about 20 items.

2. Have the students vote on the best reward items and rank them. The highest ranked items should cost the most points.

3. Copy a Point Card for each student. Each card has enough space to use this program for five hours if 10 minute intervals are used. The maximum number of signals that should be programmed per hour, however, is 30. One large Point Card is provided in the Appendix. In addition, four reduced size Point Cards are provided for ease of copying, cutting apart, and distributing to your students.

4. Initially, it is best to program about 10–15 signals per instructional hour. This should be decreased to about 2 or 3 signals when the program is working well. **Note:** Each Point Card has 30 recording intervals. If only three signals are

programmed for an instructional hour, then only three intervals would be filled in on the card and the other 27 left empty.

5. When the hour begins and a signal sounds, scan the classroom. If students are off task, instruct those students (by name) to mark an X (no points) for the interval. Praise the rest of the class for being on task and instruct them to mark a point for themselves. If you program bonus signals, then the on-task students would be instructed to mark down 2 points.

6. At the end of the day, add each student's points to his or her bank total. This is also a good time to review with students their daily progress.

7. Depending on the age of the students, hold a classroom store exchange once or twice during the week. This is where students can spend their points for the items of their choice. The cost of each item is subtracted from that student's bank total. **Hint:** One approach is to always hold an exchange on Monday (the most difficult day of the week for most students) and make the second exchange day random. This adds to the anticipation and improves performance. The number of items in the store does not need to be extensive. For instance, 15–20 items can be an adequate number.

8. At the bottom of each Point Card is a space to give points for academic performance. It is important to reward academic performance as well as on-task behavior to get the maximum performance improvement. It helps if the total number of extra points for academic performance equals to total number of points for on-task behavior (e.g., 30 signals plus 5 bonus signals = 40 on-task points and thus 40 extra points for 100% accuracy and completion).

Variation 1: If the previous approach is too complex, globally judge the academic performance of each student and give 15 points for A work, 10 points for B work, and 5 points for C work.

Variation 2: If you do not want to record extra academic performance points after each instructional period, they can be assigned at the end of the day based on your global judgment. If a total of 60 on-task points are possible across the day (15 signals x 4 instruction periods), then the global assignment might be 60 performance points for A work, 50 performance points for B work, 40 performance points for C work, and no points for below C work.

9. Reward item prices should be adjusted depending on the number of signals occurring each day. For example, if you use 15 signals for three instructional hours (or periods), the item prices should be much higher (3 times as much) than if you use only 5 signals for three instructional hours. Point costs should be adjusted when you change the number of signals for each instructional hour. **Note:** Pricing items is an art, not an exact science, and sometimes adjustments need to be based on your

judgment. Students can also be asked to help set the price of items, or a committee of students can be assigned to help make these decisions.

10. **Hint:** One approach is to have five Mystery Motivators in the classroom store along with other items. One of the five Mystery Motivators contains a highly prized reward and the other four contain common items. The students can then spend a preset high number of points to choose one of the Mystery Motivators. After a student chooses, add a new Mystery Motivator to keep the number at five.

11. **Caution:** Sometimes students will hoard points. It is best to have a zero-out exchange day about every two weeks. On this day, points that have not been spent are lost.

Beat the Secret Number Program

With this program, scan the classroom each time a signal sounds. If everyone is on task, make a hatch mark on the blackboard. If anyone is off task, indicate this and record nothing. When the number of hatch marks equals a preset secret number, the class gets a Mystery Motivator (or Spinner) at the end of the day.

Materials

Blackboard, piece of chalk, a Mystery Motivator (or Reinforcement Spinner), and a 3" x 5" index card.

Steps

1. Select a preset total number of hatch marks that the class is trying to match or beat, write it on a 3" x 5" index card, and tape it face down on the blackboard so the class cannot see the number. For example, if you are going to have four instructional periods of 15 signals per period, then the total number of signals will be 60 (4 x 15 = 60). At first, the goal can be 70–75% of the 60 signals, or about 42. When the students improve, the goal can increase to 80–85%, or about 48 signals. This should be the maximum goal. It helps to always vary the number of signals so that the goal is always changing.

2. Make a Mystery Motivator. Have the students generate some ideas for the Mystery Motivator (e.g., 15 minutes free time, having a story read to them, watching a video, popcorn party, etc.). **Hint:** Have the students generate about 20 Mystery

Motivators, about a month's supply (5 really good ones and 15 good but common ones). Write the 20 incentives on pieces of paper, put them in envelopes, and mix them up. Then use them during the next month. This enhances the anticipation because no one is sure which Mystery Motivator is going to be chosen.

3. When a signal sounds, scan the classroom. If all the students are working and on task, praise the class (sometimes it helps to praise individual students) and put a hatch mark on the blackboard. If anyone is off task, announce this and record nothing for that interval.

4. At the end of the day, if the total of hatch marks equals or exceeds the preset secret number, then the class has earned the Mystery Motivator. If the number was not reached, tell the class it was a good try and continue with your academic instruction for the period of time they would have had for the Mystery Motivator.

5. Erase the hatch marks (regardless of reaching the preset secret number) and start the process again the next day.

6. **Caution:** If one student is intentionally setting the class up to miss marks, do not let that student participate for two days. While the other students are enjoying a Mystery Motivator, this student should work on an academic assignment until he or she can participate in the system fairly.

The Get 'Em On Task Self-Management Program

This variation of the *Get 'Em On Task* program is designed to address specific problems of individual students such as out-of-seat behavior, talking out, and noisy/disruptive behaviors.

As with the previous programs, this uses the *Get 'Em On Task* program with a classroom point system. Each time a signal sounds, scan the room. If the target student(s) are not engaging in the problematic behavior, tell them to mark a point on their Point Card. If the student is engaged in the problematic behavior, tell the student to mark an X for that interval.

Once the student's behavior has improved over about a week, have the student begin to make the determination on his or her own concerning the presence or absence of the target behavior. When the signal sounds, have the student mark his or her card accordingly. Informally check student accuracy in monitoring his or her problem behaviors throughout the remainder of the program.

Materials

A 30-interval Point Card for each target student, a savings bank account where points earned are recorded by each student, and a menu of backup rewards with the number of points required to earn each reward.

Steps

1. Specifically define the behavior of concern that each target student will monitor. The definitions provided below are very precise definitions of target behaviors.

   Out-of-Seat: Getting out of seat; standing up; running; hopping; skipping; jumping; walking around; rocking in chair (without express permission).

   Talking Out: Answering teacher without raising hand or without being called on; making comments or calling out remarks when no question has been asked; calling teacher's name to get attention; crying; screaming; singing; whistling; humming; laughing loudly; coughing loudly.

   Noisy/Disruptive: Tapping pencil or other objects; clapping; tapping feet; rattling or tearing papers (only include those behaviors that you can hear with your eyes closed).

2. Teach examples of inappropriate behavior and desired alternative behaviors to the student. Role-play until you are confident the student understands the behavior(s) you have identified. This step may need to extend over a couple of sessions.

3. Use the same procedures for developing a reinforcement menu that were given previously in this manual. An important difference here, however, is that this menu is for an individual student, as opposed to a group of students. You need to be prepared to deal with complaints, such as, "that isn't fair," from other students in the class who do not have the opportunity to earn special rewards primarily because their classroom behavior is acceptable. One way to deal with this potential problem is to list a few classwide rewards on the menu that the target student can earn for his or her entire class. Extra recess or free time, a movie, a party (a high cost item), and food treats are examples of popular classwide rewards depending on the age of the students.

4. Provide a copy of the Point Card to the student. Teach the student how to mark points on the card. Again, use examples and counter examples to teach this skill to the student.

5. To start, set up the computer program with about 15–20 signals per instructional period. Decrease the number of signals to about 2–3 signals per hour when the problem behavior has essentially disappeared.

6. When a signal sounds, look at the target student. If the student is not engaged in the inappropriate behavior (e.g., talking out), tell the student to mark a point in the appropriate interval. Providing social reinforcement at the same time is a good idea (e.g., Say, "I like the way you are following the 'no talking now' rule.").

7. At the end of the instructional period or day, have the student total the number of points earned and record them on his or her Bank Points chart. Depending on the age of the student, hold a classroom store exchange once or twice per week where the student can spend the earned points for items of his or her choice.

8. You will need to check the student's self-recording accuracy. At first, you and the student should both record the student's behavior when the signal sounds. At the end of the session, compare your results to the student's results. If comparable (i.e., within plus or minus one of each other), the student gets to keep the points he/she recorded. If there is a larger discrepancy, the lower total (student's or teacher's) should be recorded in the bank account. If there are large discrepancies, it will be necessary to review the self-recording procedures with the student. Additional practice opportunities should be arranged.

9. Once the student is self-recording reliably (i.e., 8 out of 10 "matches" with your totals), tell the student that you will now let him or her do it on his or her own. However, you will still need to check the student's accuracy on a random basis. Reinforce both improved behavior and accurate self-recording.

What If I Don't Have a Computer in My Classroom?

If you do not have a computer in your classroom but have access to one, you can make cassette tapes of the computer signals and play them in your classroom. There are two methods to record the signals. You can run an audio patch cord from the computer's speaker jack to the input jack in your cassette recorder, and then run the program and record the signals. Or, simply put your recorder near the computer speaker, start the computer program, and push the record button on your cassette player. The basic drawback to this method is that you have to have the room quiet during recording or you will also record background noise. If you use either of these methods, we suggest that you make at least 3 to 5 cassette tapes (45 to 60 minutes each) with different signaling schedules. If you do not, the students will learn when the signal is about to sound and this will reduce the efficiency of the program.

How to Use This Program at Home and on the Road

At Home

The *Get 'Em On Task* program can easily be used at home, especially for behaviors that need improvement, such as homework productivity. Load the program on your home computer, select the time period for study (e.g., 60 minutes), and select the number of signals per hour (it is best to start with about 15). Each time the signal sounds, if the student is doing his or her homework, put a token (e.g., poker chip, penny, marble, or bean) in a jar. At the end of the time period, let the student exchange the tokens for a reward. An example of a simple reward is to make each token worth five minutes of television time or for staying up five minutes past an early bedtime. Tokens could also be exchanged for money, candy, earning a Mystery Motivator, or other home privileges. Whatever the student earns should not cost a lot of money or take a lot of time. It is also important to check the quality of the homework after the student has finished. If it is unacceptable, he or she should not get the reward.

Another home variation of the program is to use it to reduce teasing, fighting, or argumentative behavior. Start the program, and if during the time between signals none of this misbehavior has occurred, the family earns a token to be exchanged for something special for the whole family. For example, 20 tokens can earn a popcorn party or 30 tokens can earn a story to be read or an extra hour of television for the whole family. In this variation, earning tokens should be cumulative so that if only 15 tokens are earned in one evening, those tokens could count toward another evening's earned reward.

On the Road

Make a cassette with about 15–20 random signals per hour. Buy a couple of nickel rolls for $2.00 each (40 nickels in each roll). When you are going for an extended car trip, put the cassette in the car player. Each time a signal sounds, if there has been no misbehavior (e.g., fighting, arguing, teasing, etc.), put a nickel in a cup (or car ashtray). At the next stop, the children get to spend the nickels. In some instances, dimes or quarters may need to be used depending on the number of signals that are programmed.

A variation of this program can be used on school buses. For example, if no misbehavior occurs between signals the radio is turned on. If misbehavior occurs, the radio is turned off until the next signal. This application will require a portable cassette player because the radio is needed as the incentive. Group or in-classroom rewards can also be earned from good school bus behavior using this program.

Appendix

Suggested Reinforcers*

Reproducibles

*Lists adapted from:

Olympia, D., Andrews, D., Valum, L., & Jenson, W.R. (1993). *Homework Partners: Homework Teams.* Longmont, CO: Sopris West.

Rhode, G., Jenson, W.R., & Reavis, H.K. (1992). *The Tough Kid Book.* Longmont, CO: Sopris West.

Young, K.R., West, R.P., Smith, D.J., & Morgan, D.P. (1991). *Teaching Self-Management Strategies to Adolescents.* Longmont, CO: Sopris West.

Suggested Reinforcers

Ideas for Reinforcers For Elementary School Students

PRIVILEGES OR ACTIVITIES

- Recess (extra or longer)
- Group leader
- Go to library
- Room "manager"
- Hall monitor
- Listen to records
- Choose song in music class
- Individual conference on progress
- Field trips
- Sharpen pencil
- Read own composition to class
- No homework
- Choice of seatmate (for day, week, permanent)
- Raise flag for day or week
- Watch self on videotape
- Pass out milk
- Have parents visit
- Make gift for parent or friend
- Ride in seat behind bus driver
- Play instruments
- Crafts activities
- Head of lunch line
- Erase boards
- Go to principal's office
- After-school activity
- Tutor another pupil
- Day to chew gum in class
- Have picture taken
- Lead class in singing
- Picnic
- Cafeteria helper
- Display work to another class
- Demonstrate hobby to class
- Host in front hallway on Parent's Day
- Go home early
- Help plan daily schedule
- Collect lunch tickets
- Independent study
- Principal's help for day
- Free activity corner in room (puzzle, games)
- Perform before a group
- Help custodian
- Decorate bulletin board
- Run errands
- First or last in line
- Early dismissal
- Play game
- Help librarian
- See films
- Party
- Drink of water
- Student government activity
- Display work to principal
- Make and view videotape
- Team captain
- Select bulletin board topic
- Academic contests
- Story time
- Have lunch with teacher or principal
- Time to lie on floor, sit on desk, study outside

- Smiles, winks
- Verbal praise
- Posting picture (student of the day/week/month)
- Principal praise
- Being voted most improved student in academic area
- Eye contact

- Phone call to parents
- Pat on back
- Display self-picture
- Get to time self with stopwatch
- Physical contact (touches and squeezes)
- Homework (good papers) on bulletin board
- Being on school patrol
- Positive comments written on papers

Suggestions for Material Reinforcement for Elementary School Students

- Address book
- Art supplies
- Audio cassette tapes
- Badges
- Ball
- Balloon
- Bean bags
- Book
- Bookmark
- Bubble blowing set
- Calendar
- Chalk
- Clay or play dough
- Colored paper
- Coloring books
- Comics
- Cosmetics
- Crayons
- Eraser
- Games
- Good Student certificates
- Grab bag: toys, candy, decals
- Hackey sack
- Jacks
- Jewelry

- Jump rope
- Key chains
- Magic markers
- Marbles
- Miniature cars
- Model kits
- New pencil
- Paintbrushes/paints
- Play money
- Positive note home
- Positive phone call home
- Posters
- Puzzles
- Real money
- Rings
- School supplies
- Seasonal cards
- Self-stick skin tattoos
- Stickers
- Stuffed animals
- Surprise treats or rewards (random)
- Toiletries
- Toys
- Wax lips and teeth
- Yo-yo

Suggestions for Natural Positive Reinforcement for Elementary School Students

- Access to lunchroom snack machines (student supplies money)
- Attend school dances
- Attend school assemblies
- Be first in line (to anything)
- Be team captain
- Care for class pets
- Choose activity or game for class
- Class field trips
- Decorate the classroom
- Eat lunch in cafeteria rather than in classroom
- Extra portion at lunch
- Extra P.E., recess, or break time
- Free time to use specific equipment/supplies
- Give the student a place to display work
- Have the use of a school locker
- Help custodian
- Omit certain assignments
- Pass out paper
- Run errands
- Run film projector or video player for class
- Serve as class or office messenger or aide
- Sharpen class pencils
- Sit at teacher's desk for a specified period
- Sit by a friend
- Time with a favorite adult or peer
- Tutor in class, or with younger students
- Use of playground or P.E. equipment
- Use of class personal cassette player or tape recorder
- Use of magic markers and/or art supplies
- Visit the school library (individual or group)
- Water class plants
- Work as a lunchroom server
- Write on chalkboard (regular or colored chalk)

Ten Most-Preferred Reinforcers/Privileges

SUGGESTED FROM A SAMPLE OF HIGH SCHOOL STUDENTS

	Male Students	**Female Students**
1.	Free period (no work)	Free period
2.	In-class movie/video	Listen to music on tape
3.	Listen to music/tape	Extra grade points
4.	Extra grade points	Listen to radio
5.	Extra lunch period	Pizza party
6.	Pizza party at school	Field trips
7.	Listen to radio	Soft drinks
8.	Soft drinks in class	In-class movie
9.	Credit for gas/auto supplies	Tickets for local movies
10.	Play games on computer	Time to visit with friends

SUGGESTED FROM A SAMPLE OF HIGH SCHOOL TEACHERS

	Male Teachers	**Female Teachers**
1.	Play games with computer	Play games with computer
2.	Free period	Class field trip
3.	In-class movie/video	Free period
4.	Verbal praise from teacher	Food in class
5.	Listen to radio	Pizza party at school
6.	Positive notes home	In class movie/video
7.	Extra grade points	Listen to music on tape player
8.	Listen to music on tape player	Verbal praise
9.	Fast food coupons	Listen to radio
10.	Tickets for movies	Tickets for movies

List of All Reinforcers Chosen at Least Once by At-Risk and Special Education Secondary Students

- Skiing
- Bowling
- Baseball
- Swimming
- Pool
- Soccer
- Horse ride
- Skating
- Golf
- Biking
- Football
- Weightlift
- Fish
- Basketball
- Tennis
- Gymnastics
- Hunting
- Dancing
- Running
- Gym pass
- Skateboarding
- Airplane
- Field trip
- Shopping
- Take picture
- Assemblies
- Movie video
- Computer
- Art gallery
- Music lesson
- Chew gum
- Talk/visit
- Have class with friend
- Cook in class
- Build models
- Draw
- Go to park
- Sleep

- Free absence
- No homework
- Miss test
- A/100%
- Free time
- Choose own seat
- Longer lunch
- Leave early
- Miss assignment
- Teacher/office aide
- Early lunch
- Parking
- Shorter class
- Name on board
- Free time with friend
- Gift certificate
- Class outside
- Copy of good work
- Video games
- Book/magazine
- Visit arcade
- Cash
- Board games
- Watch
- Bingo
- Arcade token
- Game hour
- Colored pen
- Class party
- Sunglasses
- Pizza party
- Stuffed animal
- Mug
- Poster
- Pop
- Jewelry
- Popcorn
- Jumper cables

- Ice cream
- Baseball cards
- T-shirts
- Candy
- Movie ticket
- Doughnuts
- Wallet
- Fries
- Hairdo
- Food
- Health/beauty aids
- Concert tickets
- Gas/car supplies
- Hair spray
- Auction
- Notebook
- Tape
- Campfire with hot dogs
- Drumsticks
- Snack break
- Praise
- Fruit
- Art supplies
- Skateboard stickers
- Grab bag
- Calendar
- Eat with friend
- Computer disk
- Picnic
- Record
- Group out to eat
- Skateboard items
- Laminate work
- Road sign
- Headphones
- Perfume

Reproducibles

Point Card

Name: _____

1	2	3	4	5
6	7	8	9	10
11	12	13	14	15
16	17	18	19	20
21	22	23	24	25
26	27	28	29	30

Academic Points: _____

Behavior: _____

Date: _____

Point Card

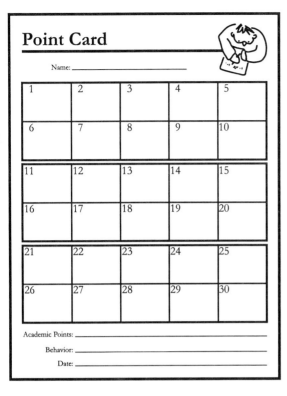

Name: _____

1	2	3	4	5
6	7	8	9	10
11	12	13	14	15
16	17	18	19	20
21	22	23	24	25
26	27	28	29	30

Academic Points: _____

Behavior: _____

Date: _____

Point Card

Name: _____

1	2	3	4	5
6	7	8	9	10
11	12	13	14	15
16	17	18	19	20
21	22	23	24	25
26	27	28	29	30

Academic Points: _____

Behavior: _____

Date: _____

Point Card

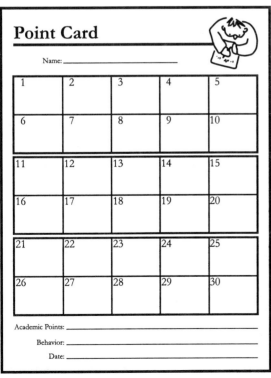

Name: _____

1	2	3	4	5
6	7	8	9	10
11	12	13	14	15
16	17	18	19	20
21	22	23	24	25
26	27	28	29	30

Academic Points: _____

Behavior: _____

Date: _____

Point Card

Name: _____

1	2	3	4	5
6	7	8	9	10
11	12	13	14	15
16	17	18	19	20
21	22	23	24	25
26	27	28	29	30

Academic Points: _____

Behavior: _____

Date: _____

Behavior Observation Form

Target Student			M/F	Grade
School		Teacher		Date
Observer		Position		

Class Activity

Teacher directed whole class   Teacher directed small group   Independent work session

Directions: Each box represents a ten-second interval. Observe each student once; then record the data. This is a partial interval recording. If possible, collect data for the full 15 minutes under a teacher directed or independent condition. If this is not possible, put a slash when the classroom condition changes. Classmates observed must be the same sex as the target student.

	1									2									3
Target Student																			
Peer*																			

	4									5									6
Target Student																			
Peer*																			

	7									8									9
Target Student																			
Peer*																			

	10									11									12
Target Student																			
Peer*																			

	13									14									15
Target Student																			
Peer*																			

* Randomly selected classmate of the same sex

Note: To observe class, begin with the first same sex student in row 1. Record each subsequent same sex student in following intervals. Data reflect an average of classroom behavior. Skip unobservable students.

On-Task Codes
    Eye contact with teacher or task and performing the requested task.

Off-Task Codes
    T = **Talking Out/Noise** (Inappropriate verbalization or making sounds with object, mouth, or body)
    O = **Out of Seat** (Student fully or partially out of assigned seat without teacher permission)
    I = **Inactive** (Student not engaged with assigned task and passively waiting, sitting, etc.)
    N = **Noncompliance** (Breaking a classroom rule or not following teacher directions within 15 seconds)
    P = **Playing With Object** (Manipulating objects without teacher permission)
    + = **Positive Teacher Interaction** (One-on-one positive comment, smiling, touching, or gesture)
    – = **Negative Teacher Interaction** (One-on-one reprimand, implementing negative consequence, or negative gesture)
    / = **Neutral Teacher Interaction** (One-on-one expressionless teacher interaction, no approval or disapproval expressed, directions given)

Reprinted with permission from Jenson, W.R., Rhode, G., and Reavis, H.K. (1994). *The Tough Kid Tool Box.* Longmont, CO: Sopris West.

Yes and No Cards

YES	YES	YES	YES
NO	NO	NO	NO
YES	YES	YES	YES
NO	NO	NO	NO
YES	YES	YES	YES
NO	NO	NO	NO

Reinforcement Spinner

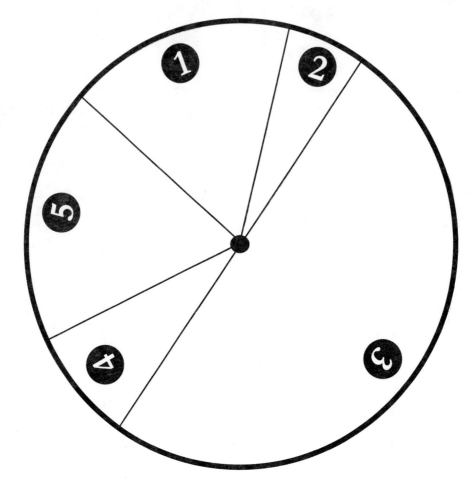

Reward Menu

1 _____

2 _____

3 _____

4 _____

5 _____

Points

Name	Mon	Tue	Wed	Thur	Fri	Total